Then & Now

RHONDDA FAWR

This bronze group statue was commissioned by the Rhondda Civic Society, showing a miner, his wife and baby, who is being nursed 'Welsh' fashion, with a wrap-around shawl. The sculptor is Robert Thomas. The statue was unveiled on 14 October 1993 by Viscount Tonypandy, former speaker of the House of Commons. It is positioned on the site of the one-time Glamorgan collieries, which is historically associated with the Tonypandy Riots of 1910. The group statue commemorates the communities of Rhondda who, through hard work, managed to triumph over adversity and made the Rhondda known and respected throughout the world.

The rise of the Rhondda came during the second half of the nineteenth century, marking the tremendous pace of sweeping industrialisation. After 1850 the coal rush was on. News of the new Klonoyke travelled fast, attracting mine venturers and settlers from far and wide. Miners and ironworkers arrived on foot, and the pack-horse brought more from the western valleys of Monmouthshire, Merthyr and Somerset, increasing the immigrant population during the succeeding years and transforming the Rhondda from green rural to black industrial. The new settlers were to become known as the 'Valley Boys', rough characters eager to escape the old way of life for the new. Few discovered the route to the instant 'good life', but they would not have missed the adventure they did find for anything in the world. A vast transformation had begun, bringing the total number of settlers in the parish up from 550 in 1800 to 169,000 by the year 1903.

Then & Now

RHONDDA FAWR

Alan Phillips

TEMPUS

To Jean

The Author

Alan Phillips is a native of Penygraig in the Rhondda Fawr valley. He attended Graid-Yr-Eos Secondary Boy's School and Gwent College of Higher Education and is a keen local historian with various writings and works to his credit. In his early life he was recognised for his tenure as Branch Secretary, District Board Delegate (vice chairman) and Conference Delegate for B.F. & A.W.U. and was directly involved with two national strikes in the baking industry. He served with the Royal Regiment of Wales Tavr and ACR (Sergeant Instructor) at home and abroad. Alan Phillips married Jean Sparrow from Ystrad and has two sons and a daughter. He is presently employed in leisure and tourism with Rhondda-Cynon-Taff at Maes-Yr-Haf Community Centre Services in Trealaw, Rhondda.

THE ARMORIAL BEARINGS
OF THE
BOROUGH OF RHONDDA
Granted by Letters Patent 1955.

HWY·CLOD·NA·GOLUD

First published 2003

Tempus Publishing Limited
The Mill, Brimscombe Port,
Stroud, Gloucestershire, GL5 2QG

British Library Cataloguing in Publication Data.
A catalogue record for this book is available from the British Library.

ISBN 0 7524 2843 8

Typesetting and origination by Tempus Publishing Limited
Printed in Great Britain by Midway Colour Print, Wiltshire

CONTENTS

FOREWORD

The Rhondda valleys have been said to be the most famous of their kind in the world; they certainly played a major part in the industrial development of the United Kingdom. In the nineteenth century they rapidly changed from an idyllic, peaceful and rural setting to an altogether different place of vibrant, congested turmoil riddled with scores of coal mines.

Now the valleys are reverting to their original state, and they have the added bonus of the Rhondda people, who have developed over this history, their homes, communities, institutions and traditions.

Alan Phillip's book traces this story and, combing words and visual images, conjures up the past and serves us a reminder of our history. It is a history of toil and struggle against a backdrop of comradeship, love of neighbour, self-help and our wonderful valley tapestry of music, drama, religious commitment and sport.

Thank you, Alan, for your commitment to our ever-changing, ever-special Rhondda valleys.

Allan Rogers, MP for Rhondda 1983-2001

ACKNOWLEDGEMENTS

I wish to express my gratitude to all the staff of Rhondda-Cynon-Taff libraries and patrons of Rhondda Camera Club, Maes-Yr-Haf Community Centre and Dan Murphy Day Centre for allowing me the use of old photographs throughout this book. I am indebted to Lawrie Saurin for the photographs taken from his private collection and to Gwyn Evans, Jack Farr and Liz Gulley; also to Aldo Bacchetta, Ivor (Pete) Bartlett, Wayne Carter, Allen Davies, Lyn Elias, Brian Flowers, Lynn Jones, and Les Lewis for their help. Thanks are also due to Flair Studios, Porth, and in particular Allan Rogers, for writing the forward with real strength and openness, and to Amy Rigg and Fran Gannon at Tempus Publishing for their enthusiasm and support. I'd like to say another big thank you to the South Wales Police, for all their help at Tonypandy Police Station.

Finally, I give my warmest thanks and much appreciation to my daughter Samantha Jane for classifying the material and spending so much time on various aspects of the project, and to my wife Jean for assisting me in my work at photographic locations throughout the Fawr Valley.

INTRODUCTION

Over the past decades and up to our present time, many have come to Rhondda,
have stayed and prospered.

The Rhondda has two rivers, the Rhondda Fawr (large) and Rhondda Fach (small),
running southward. Between the two Rhondda's lies the ridge of Cefn Rhondda. From
Treherbert in the Fawr and Maerdy in the Fach, the rivers flow until they meet at
Porth. Here (called the Gateway to the Rhondda) the two rivers meet and merge as
one, becoming the River Rhondda, which continues on to Pontypridd to meet the
River Taff.

This book celebrates the Rhondda Fawr, reflecting a chain link of twenty-seven
townships compiled into chapters. It illustrates many examples of buildings
characteristic of Welsh industrial development, and relates the changes that have
occurred in the valleys from the beginnings of the coal era up to the present time.
These pages take the reader on a journey through the camera lens, capturing in some
small measure the overall picture of Rhondda Fawr both then and now, with a
special reminder of the King Coal era.

The modern pictures show many impressions of the very different life we
experience in the Rhondda today, and prove that the Rhondda people's resilience,
adaptability and desire for change remains ever constant and must ultimately find its
expression. It would seem from the account given in these photographs and
commentaries that in the Rhondda an appreciation of the legacy bequeathed to us by
bygone ages is still very strong.

From Pillar Stall to Longwall, hundreds of thousands of men were employed to
dig for coal for a great number of products, a process that was to progress almost
uninterrupted to culminate in worldwide recognition. The name Rhondda spread
throughout the coal industry as the greatest steam coal-exporting centre in the world
and undoubtedly accelerated technological innovation, expanding markets, causing
rapid population growth and increased wealth. Before this happened the Rhondda's
were little known to outside people, until the discovery of coal in the lower strata of
Rhondda was quickly extended to the upper strata and the great change ensued.

When the early speculators arrived there were only a small number of scattered hill
farms and labourers cottages marking the efforts of human life, the chief industries
being wood production, rearing sheep or cattle, or working at the woollen mill at
Tonypandy. Here, alongside the preachers of the Methodist cause, the engaging coal
industry and its workers forged the history of King Coal.

The first immigrants came to Dinas and gradually created a settlement on a considerable scale in the parish of Llantrisant. The great historian Morien wrote in 1803 about the engaging coal industry, meaning early coal mining, showing Dinas during uncertain times and recalling Dinas settlers assembled in the largest cottages for spiritual teaching. When these proved too small they would assemble in the outhouses or barns, to hold prayer meetings and to enrol themselves into what they call, and still call, Societies. One of the early chapels built by the Welsh reformers was Ebenezer Dinas. It was built within a stone's throw from the swift-running River Rhondda at the foot of Dinas Mountain. The chapel was built at the foot of Carn-Y-Celyn Mountain, among scattered labourer's cottages, in the locality now called Penygraig.

We can argue that this kind of religious discipline was in reality a form of class control by which the workers could be prevented from exercising any form of strong challenge to the mine owners. Essentially the portrayal becomes one of a people resisting repression. Welsh chapels captured the new industrial spectator and became the means by which ordinary people organized their lives, interacting and influencing directly or indirectly any worthy aims. Above all else the chapels provided means and encouragement for people to learn how to read and write as a result of Sunday school instruction.

Walter Coffin was the first successful mining engineer in the Lower Rhondda, sinking his first deep mine in the village of Dinas. To recognise his initial involvement and what followed, we must examine what is now a strictly imaginary scene of pre-industrial Rhondda. It is worthwhile considering the environment of Morien, who penned at a time in which the valley still retained its pastoral character. The only highway through the bottom of the valley was narrow and generally flanked by tall hedgerows. At intervals there were rustic gates across it, indicating farm boundaries. Also nearby slopes were lined with grey dry walls, which served the same purpose as the gates. Morien wrote about well-spaced farmhouses, each one with green fields adjacent to it, and each year in September there might be seen the occasional cornfield, bright in the sunshine. Through the bottom of the valley was the Little Rhondda (Frisky), a name corrupted to Rhondda River, its waters pure as crystal and in which might be seen fleets of the pink spotted trout with their silver sheen.

The documentary sources, whether primary or secondary, tell us of an early community that was extremely bright and sharp-witted, but which at the same time lacked any education in the modern sense of the word. English was almost as little known then as Latin is today. It was a little world in itself, standing apart. It was the landscape of Morien that Walter Coffin came upon in 1804, when he arrived to sink the first deep mine.

Alan Phillips

Chapter 1

PORTH AND TREHAFOD BORDER

A picture of a postcard painting from the early twentieth century, of the top of the upper shop façades, bearing the letters 'T and E', the initials of Thomas and Evans store. In 1888 the partnership came to an end. William Thomas had his interest for business in Aberbeeg; William Evans remained in Porth, prospered and built an empire. Outstandingly successful industrialist, wholesaler and retailer that he was, he was also known for his public benefactions and made Porth familiar to all parts of Britain with his famous 'Corona' drinks and crown logo.

Bronwyod House, Porth, once the home of William Evans, the great Welsh industrialist. A French architect designed it in the 1920s. *The Rhondda Leader* referred to him as a Welsh industrial prince, a man whose influence on Rhondda and Porth in particular has scarcely been equalised.

Outwardly at least, the house looks today much as it did during William Evans' time. The difference is on the inside; today rebuilt, it has multipurpose office rooms for Rhondda-Cynon-Taff administration staff workers.

Porth Hospital in the lower Rhondda, 1894-1999, opened as a result of miner's subscriptions and benefactors such as Dr Henry Nauton Davies, who had led a team of nine men during the Tynewydd Colliery disaster in 1877. The mine was inundated with water from the old workings of the nearby Upper Cymmer Colliery. Fourteen men were trapped, four of these were drowned and one was killed by the rush of compressed air during a rescue attempt of the nine survivors. Four were released after eighteen hours and the remaining five after a nine-day struggle. Under Dr Davies and his team the rescued men were taken to the Tynewydd Inn, where beds had been prepared for them. Twenty-one years previously this very same room had been the scene of the first big explosion in the Rhondda, when 114 lives were lost. The new cottage hospital greatly improved the medical facilities for the people of Rhondda.

Nowadays, modern needs replace the old. The site is being made ready for a new structure and purpose, occupying the grounds where Porth Hospital once stood.

Hannah Street, Porth, with people gathering for the opportunity of taking part in a photography shoot, in the early years of the twentieth century. Today people can still walk freely down the street, but there is often bumper-to-bumper car parking on the road. Hannah Street boasts a wide selection of small independent retailers and special interest shops, restaurants and homely cafés. Not a lot has changed here since the old days. The fence on the right of the present-day picture incoporates ground belonging to the former Salam chapel.

The modern picture shows Station Street, near Porth Square, with Lloyds Bank and Porth Hotel at the entrance. Various shopkeepers subsequently occupied the bank. In the distant background is Porth railway station, standing in evidence of the name of the street.

Taken from near the same position, the old photograph shows Station Street at the turn of the century, an informative and thought-provoking picture. The shops that run uninterrupted down both sides of the street are rather less elegant than those shops situated in the commercial or middle-class residential areas during this era. This picture was taken long before the old roads were improved and new roads contructed in this area of town. It was largely due to the efforts of Sir D. Lleufer Thomas that the need for better road

communications was fully appreciated and a comprehensive scheme put into place during the early 1920s. But by the end of 1924 the industrial boom had collapsed, and there now began for the Rhondda townships a period of persistent depression, which lasted until the outbreak of the Second World War.

Porth and Ystrad, respectively, were the first railway stations to be built in Rhondda. By 1861 the first passenger service was opened in Rhondda to meet the rapid rise in population, following the increased demand for coal.

Today, much of the railway is undergoing profound change, with a great deal of the rail network steadily being replaced by motorways. Rhondda still has a small number of stations connected at Treherbert, Treorchy, Ystrad Rhondda, Llwynypia, Tonypandy, Dinas, Porth and Trehafod, all of which operate to mainline stations.

Cymmer Bridge was built in 1893, and reconstructed and widened in 1924. Its maker was the Hoseway Co. Ltd, Shropshire, designed and directed by the staff of the Rhondda Urban District Council, Porth.

Here can also be seen Porth during less causative times, with the old footbridge in the foreground; the large house on the right was the residence of Dr Naunton Davies. The stone bridge was rebuilt in 1764, by joint contributions from the parishes of Llantrisant and Ystradyfodwg, and cost annually from £20 to £30 to maintain. Most bridges at this time were of wooden structure. The bridge in the new picture is the original 1924 reconstruction, and is still in use today.

This is Pioneer Food Market, Porth, a Co-operative Group (CWS). This was a site occupied by a number of George Insole's collieries between 1886 and 1940. The last colliery opened in 1856 and was leased to T.C. Hinde.

It was at Cymmer Colliery on 15 July 1856 that 160 men and boys were almost at their places of work underground when an explosion occurred. It was first reported that every man and boy must certainly be dead, but it was found that some miners were still in the area near the pit bottom and had survived. The death toll was 114.

Gummers grocers, loading deliveries with horse and cart in the Pontypridd Road, near Porth Square. The year is 1910, a time when shopping centres were well established in every town in the two Rhondda Valleys. Both large and small businesses grew together, providing ample opportunities in the Rhondda for a life in the trade of a businessman.

Pontypridd Road today symbolises a less flourishing town, due to the new and very different way of life afforded by the family car and increasingly popular out-of-town shopping.

Serious rail accidents were rare in Rhondda. This one occurred on 23 January 1911, between the Trehafod Border and Pontypridd. The train left Treherbert station at 9.10 a.m. bound for Cardiff and would soon smash into the rear end of a stationary coal train, at a place known as the Coke Ovens; eleven passengers were killed in the event. The last passengers boarded the ill-fated train from the villages of Trehafod and Hopskinstown, and the almighty impact followed within seconds.

The modern photograph is Trehafod station, with the new entrance to the passenger train platform.

A rare image of the public swimming pool in Bronwydd Park, 1930. The park was established by the Rhondda District Council. The park, with its extensive sporting and recreational facilities for all ages, was built on ground purchased by William Evans, the founder of Thomas and Evans' Welsh hills soft drink empire and a recognised public servant and Christian philanthropist. He offered the two hundred acres of ground adjoining Coeocae Field, Porth, at a cost of £3,500, for conversion into a public park.

In 1994 the existing outdoor pool was converted to an indoor one with a sliding roof, erected by Amery Buildings in conjunction with Rhondda Borough Council. The pool was opened on 4 March 1995, by the Mayor of Rhondda Councillor, Brian Rowlands, followed by a group of council VIPs, all very much impressed by the new facilities.

The group of ladies in the new picture are undergoing swimming instruction and all smiling radiantly. Instructors at the pool are well trained in teaching skills to swimmers of all abilities, from the very beginning, getting into the water, progressing to breast stroke and back stroke and even diving, all under the watchful eyes of the lifeguards.

Chiesa, near Bardi. This thriving family business continues to progress under the two sons, seen here in the modern picture, with a member of staff. Aldo Bacchetta is on the left and Ron Baccheta on the right. Now called Bachetta's Coffee Shop and Delicatessen, the place has grown from just one property to three, knocked into one large redevelopment.

At first glance upon entry the current shop looks much like the original, which had all the characteristics of early Italian cafés. One note of interest, all Italian cafés here were long referred to as Bracchis, after Angelo Bracchi, the first Italian in the Rhondda in the early 1890s – he opened a café in Tonypandy!

The Station Café in Station Street, Porth, originally established in 1932 thanks to the efforts of two Italian immigrants, Serafino Bacchetta from Bardi and his wife, Dornito from

Lewis Merthyr Colliery, Trehafod, founded in 1873 and closed in 1983. It was purchased by William Lewis (Lord Merthyr). Two shafts were sunk and named the Bertie and Trevor, after his sons. This became one of the largest producing collieries in the Rhondda.

Disaster struck on 22 November 1956 due to a large pocket of gas which ignited by a fall of stone in the No. 4 district in the two feet nine inches seam. Two men were killed outright, seven men later died of their injuries, and five men were also injured. At the time of the explosion there were 936 men employed underground.

The new Heritage Park Hotel, built on the cold colliery site, the stack, – the only one remaining in Rhondda – stands as a reminder of the coal industry, reminiscent of the old customs and traditions of Rhondda past.

Porth Square, pictured on a Sunday in 1953. Buses arrive from Maerdy, in the centre of the square, and from Treherbert, to the far left. In the middle of the roundabout there is a telephone box and public toilets – now demolished for safety reasons – and near to the bus stop can be seen the district war memorial, which was erected on the river bank in 1928 in memory of those who gave their lives in the First World War. The post office building is on the right. The modern picture is the same scene taken in the winter of 1985, looking much as it did before.

Chapter 2

DINAS AND TREALAW

Dinas in 1904, the first coal pioneering town in Rhondda Fawr due to the ventures of Dr Richard Griffiths in the 1790s and Walter Coffin in the early nineteenth century. By the time this photograph was taken Dinas had lost its earlier picture-book charm. After 1840 there was a rapid economic growth in the district that eventually spread to the middle and upper reaches of the valley, creating what would be phenomenal expansion in the industrial development of the Rhondda. Here there was a transformation, from a secluded pastoral area of small hill farms into a huge mining Klondike inhabited by a new industrial class.

The Mines Rescue Station, Riverside Villas, Appletree, Dinas. The station was officially opened by King George V and Queen Mary on 27 June 1912. The men in the old picture form No. 1 Rescue Squad, as they were in 1914. Left to right, back row: W.E. Emerson M.E. (captain), H. Davies, Daniel Roberts, Superintendent Thorne. Front row: T. Comm, Cornelius Gronow and Robert Roberts.

The station today is manned with eighteen regular staff and a rescue officer. All of them reside in Appletree with their families. From left to right, front row: Andrew Griffiths (brigadesman); Bob McDonald (asst. manager); Adrian Scourfield (deputy manager); Lyn Elias (manager); Mark Tibbet (rescue officer); David Michael (brigadesman); Ray Lusty (brigadesman). Middle row: Adrian Rowlands, Les Morris, Tim Carrey, Rob England, Mike Llewellyn (brigadesmen). Back row: Lyndon Jones, Kevin Griffiths, Rob Carter (brigadesmen).

A damaged picture of Dinas railway station, 1940. Today it remains open but consists of only one platform and a very small shelter for the passenger single-line service on the up or down train.

The 1963 Beechings Report on railways led to the closure of over 300 branch lines throughout Wales. Despite strong opposition from the affected area, cuts continued. In Rhondda Fawr every village station from Porth to Maerdy was ultimately to close under the controversial reorganisation of the railways.

The old photograph is of Maes-Yr-Haf Community Centre in 1951, for the Festival of Britain celebrations which marked the centenary of the Great Exhibition of 1851. The modern picture shows Maes-Yr-Haf Community Centre in 2001; it was formerly the educational settlement, and has played an outstanding part in the provision of cultural facilities and social activities throughout the Rhondda. It was visited by King George VI and Queen Elizabeth in 1941. Maes-Yr-Haf settlement was the only one of its kind in South Wales. Its creation and ensuing growth is undoubtedly due to the efforts of the Quaker Society of Friends. The settlement snowballed from small beginnings to a position widely held to be essential in providing adult education for the people of Rhondda.

Today Maes-Yr-Haf Community Centre is the responsibility of the Rhondda-Cynon-Taff Council and still embraces all aspects of community life.

The Royal Hotel situated next door to the Maes-Yr-Haf Community Centre on the Brithwaunydd Road in Trealaw district. This hotel was built in 1895 and its first landlord was Mr Jenkin Williams. The old photograph was taken in 1910; this was the year when the people showed great solidarity and a solid determination to fight injustice and shape a better future for the valley communities, the time of the 1910/11 pit dispute.

The new photograph was taken in 1999. The present owner, Mr Patrick Taylor and his manager, Steve Allen, keep a traditional hotel with modern en-suite bathrooms and utility rooms. The ornate canopy over the front entrance to the hotel was taken away for the war effort and has never been replaced.

The Miskin Hotel in 1910, standing between Trealaw Road on the left and Miskin Road on the right, in a northerly direction towards Mid-Rhondda and the upper reaches of the valley in the village of Blaenrhondda. The hotel was built in 1875 and its first landlord was Mr Robert Williams. The Rhondda had a great number of public houses per head of the population during those days.

Under the present-day landlords, Ian and Kath Harges, the Miskin Hotel is still very busy, and drinking beer is still much preferred to drinking water, milk or tea!

S lum clearance, spearheaded by Rhondda Borough Council during the late 1960s redevelopment scheme. The old photograph shows the very last glimpse of nineteenth-century Dinas. Until the bulldozers arrived, Graig Ddu and Gwaun Adda Dinas was full of community life, a place where people worked and lived side by side in the shadow of the colliery. Near the 4th pole in the centre of the old photograph is a concrete slab where the first shaft was sunk in Rhondda. It all began in 1807, when a man named Walter Coffin arrived by horse track. He was the second son of Walter Coffin and his wife Anne, a very rich and respected family from Nolton, Brigend. The young Walter was fresh out of the academy at Exeter and now he began seeking mineral selections in the lower Rhondda Fawr. He made his venture a success as a pioneer in Dinas, Trealaw and the surrounding land. He hauled and marketed coal, beginning the first industrial settlement in Rhondda. Coffin became known as 'King Coal', sowing the seeds of the industry that would provide for generations to come.

Today stands a new Dinas. The block of flats on the left in the new photograph, named Pen-Dinas, runs alongside part of the Glen level incline near and below Graig Ddu, where Coffin resolved to sink his first shaft.

An artist's impression of Dinas Colliery explosion, 1879. The colliery consisted of two pits, the lower and middle pit, the downcast and upcast. Only six out of sixty-three bodies were recovered.

Coal had long been mined in the South Wales regions, although there was very little expansion before the eighteenth century. Welsh coal mines greatly influenced the development of iron making. Records show that coal was being mined in the Kilvey area, near Swansea, during the mid-fourteenth century. Pocket coal mining expanded a little by the sixteenth century in the Gower, Margam Abby and the Vale of Glamorgan at Brynmenin, Llanharry and Pentyrch. Small but favourable amounts of coal were found at Hirwalin, Dowlais and Senghenyod.

Paul R. Davies in his archaeological account of industrial sites in Rhondda informed his readers of outcrops of coal mined at Rhigos and Glyn Rhondda in 1612. He mentions Hurs estate map of 1717, which shows coal workings at Trebanog. In early mining operations, surface seams were little more than a drift dropping from one to twenty feet deep. Dinas in the lower Rhondda made industrial history in 1807 due chiefly to Walter Coffin's first colliery at Graig Ddu in Dinas.

The deep working mine suffered greater danger from rock falls, flooding and fire damp. Those who survived the explosions and rock falls usually became old and sick before their time.

Chapter 3

PENYGRAIG AND WILLIAMSTOWN

Unemployed and old age pensioners annual outing, 28 July 1936. Some were on crutches as a result of injury in the First World War. Many of the old timers were born and grew up during Rhondda's great expansion of the coal industry and the problems that came out of its demands that were not so easily overcome. Still, all were looking strong for the camera and ready for the off, come rain or shine.

In those days the Mecca day trip for Rhondda folk was Barry Island or Porthcawl, both resorts being beside the seaside. These trips were a boon that provided sheer magic for all ages.

Brook Street, Williamstown in 1909, the year of the 'People's Budget' under Lloyd George's government. The children gathered in the street are probably interested in the camera, an unusual visitor. Upon reaching ten years of age, the boys pictured here might well have been employed in the coal industry. The census figures from 1901 to 1931 show sixty-eight per cent of the children here entered into coal mining, or a subsidiary industry connected to coal.

The modern picture is the same street but in 2003, now a very quiet area in which to live, inhabited mostly by older residents. Most of the shops are now closed down, and there are very few left from the beginning of the century.

A view of Penygraig taken from Trealaw Road. The Sports Ground (RFC) is the site of the Old Naval Colliery coal yard. The naval collieries materialised into development control companies during the late 1870s; rich steam coal seams made rapid returns with profits going to the masters of the coalfields. Naval collieries opened first, the Pandy Pit opened in 1879 and sold out to the new naval companies in 1887.

In 1910 the new owners opened the Anthony Pit. Both pits rest on or near the border between Tonypandy and Penygraig. At this time, the new steam coal collieries became part of the Cambrian Combine. In the same year a great deal of unrest spread throughout the coalfields. This was a time that has been well documented in Welsh history.

A postcard of Penygraig Road, Penygraig 1912. The building on the left and near to the bend is the Labour Progressive Club, Penygraig. Established in 1904, it was rebuilt in 1912. A very popular club in present-day Rhondda, it boasts a serious commitment to membership and provides all the right facilities for public entertainment. The new picture shows a different view today, with a road to the left where shops once stood, which meets up with the new roundabout. The building on the left is the Labour Club in 2003.

Two street parties; the old picture is Library Road during what Churchill described as a 'brief period of rejoicing' – Victory in Europe Day, 8 May 1945. Celebrations swept the country, adults partying well into the night, dancing and singing in the street. For the children in the photograph, the sweetness of victory was in the jelly.

The new photograph is of Mikado Street during the investiture of Charles, Prince of Wales. The ceremony took place at Caernarfon Castle on 1 July 1969. There were not so many people out in the streets celebrating that day, but, an indication of changing times, five hundred million television viewers all over the world watched the investiture.

Tylacelyn Rd., Penygraig, Rhondda. 3060.

Tylycelyn Road, Penygraig, the shopping centre during the forties. This was then a small valley town of 6,800 people. During Rhondda's peak concentration of population, between 1881 and 1911, Penygraig housed 8,400 people and made a great contribution the development of the Rhondda. Although there are fewer people around now and most shop at the supermarkets, there are still a number of well-established shops on Penygraig main street, sharing a mutual interest in the market for business.

A Rhondda family outing – a welcome day trip at Coney Beach, Porthcawl 1952. This was the same year in which the people's King died unexpectedly and a newly crowned Queen signified the coming of a new age. The little girl in the old picture is from a generation of 'New Elizabethans'.

The later photograph is a picture of a Rhondda family on a similar day trip in 1981, proving that some things, happily, will never change. The 'Flash, Bank what a picture' was taken on the same day as the wedding of Lady Diana Spencer to the Prince of Wales. It was the beginnings of a kind of public mania and deep love for Diana, and the event perhaps explains the small number of people on the beach that day.

Looking up Tylacelyn Road from the square in around 1955, in the early days of retailing television sets, as can be seen on the sign for Rowetts shop on the right. On the left-hand side of the road, almost out of sight, stands the Industrial Co-operative Society, opened in 1914 under Mr Henshaw, the chairman. Penygraig C.W.S. started up with forty-six people in 1891 and grew to boast 6,200 members by 1937. The Blackbook 'Divi' (dividend) was paid back to members when there was a surplus on trade and was a very popular means of saving. Today a brand new library stands on the former site of the Co-operative stores.

The Square, Penygraig, 1957. Almost every building in the photograph was incorporated in a large demolition programme to reshape the Rhondda during the seventies and to make way for a for a new roundabout. The large building with the tree in front is Soar Ffwroamas, built in 1832. The chapel made room for the Penygraig Community Project, opened by Prince Charles in 1978. Also known as 'Valley Kids', it originated in a two-roomed basement owned by the Co-operative Society at Cross Street.

Tylacelyn Road, leading to Tonypandy, pictured here in 1980. On the far left of the old picture is the Penygraig RFC's clubhouse, formerly the naval colliery manager's house. On the right is the entrance to what used to be the Penygraig Naval Colliery and Rhondda Urban District Council waste disposal tip in 1940. Now it is the site of Penygraig's RFC ground, called Graig Park, and home to what is a very well respected and popular club throughout the country.

The Llantrisant train leaving Penygraig during the days of the Great Western Railways. The service originated during the period described in the history books as that of the 'railway mania' and in 1864 a rival company to the then Taff Vale Railway was incorporated under the Rhondda and Ely Valleys Junction Railway Company. The new railway ran a broad-gauge line from Blaenrhondda to Penygraig and Ely Valley, which was later re-routed to take in Cwm Clydach. Also diesel rail cars worked from here during the fifties as carriers of passengers and freight, before Rhondda's fast dying branch lines finally passed into appreciated history.

As can be seen in the later photograph, nothing remains from the old days. The new A4119 access road for the M4 motorway is now firmly in place, running over the old Taff Vale railway track.

The old picture is of Tonypandy Elementary School in around 1920, looking gaunt, Victorian and over-powering. It was built in 1915.

Before the 1870 education act incorporated the school board system, Rhondda, situated in the parish of Ystradyfodwg, used the parish vestry system to control elementary education throughout the districts and continued to enforce this long after the education department attempted to change the system. However, the rapidly changing industrial and social situations in the Rhondda and the steering towards a system of enlightened self-help eventually established a strong school board system. Soon teaching was 'chalk and talk' and learning the three R's. Secondary education was preached by many to herald the beginnings of what would ultimately mean great advancement for Rhondda's youth. The long-established traditional system of education now actively implements the principles of comprehensive education, and is a system still very much motivated by the aspirations of the pupils.

The old elementary school above is now Tonypandy Comprehensive School, seen here in 2002. The school has been awarded the Charter Mark. The Charter Mark is the Government's award scheme for recognising and encouraging excellence in public services. It has been a very successful and rewarding time for the school's head-teacher, Mrs Parry, assistant-head Mrs Helen O'Sullivan, and all of the pupils and staff.

Chapter 4

TONYPANDY AND CLYDACH VALE

A fountain and water trough erected at Tonypandy Square in memory of Archibald Hood, a great Scots mining engineer. He ran two mining companies, the Lothian Coal Company in Midlothian and the Glamorgan Coal Company in Rhondda. Hood's achievements in Rhondda are without comparison.

Archibald Hood was born in Kilmarnock, Ayrshire, on 4 June 1823, the oldest son of Robert Hood, a colliery overman. His mother died when he was very young. On reaching the age of thirteen, he began his working life in charge of surface engines at the local colliery, working twelve hours a day. He had a great desire to improve himself, pareticularly in mining and geological mattrs, and was soon to qualify as an engineer. Within a few short years he reached the appointed position of chief mineral agent and engineer of the South Wales coal fields.

The huts, Tonypandy, seen here in around 1950. They were built in 1862 for Archibald Hood to house his pit sinkers at the Glamorgan Colliery, and were demolished to make way for the new Mitchell Court Development, named after Alderman Sydney Mitchell. The three men sat on the bench are Rhondda transport workers, probably drivers or conductors during the fifties.

The new picture is of the same station forty years later, when Stagecoach was beginning its bus service.

Dunraven Street, Tonypandy, in around 1900, back when the roads were rough and uneven in wet weather. The shops on the right with the awnings in place have long since been replaced by a shopping complex. The modern photograph was taken during the summer of 1999, and shows the inside of the precinct where there is an area for parents and children on a 'fun-day'. The building was officially opened by Rt. Hon. Nicholas Edwards M.P., Secretary for Wales, on 10 September 1986.

Dunraven Street, Tonypandy, in around 1914. The old picture affords us a view of much activity, on what appears to be a busy shopping day. It is generally accepted that from 1900 to 1914 employment in the Rhondda was fairly constant. Any rise in the wages of the average family was particularly noticeable in the shopping centre.

Dunraven is still very much a bustling shopping street today, and is now a pedestrianized area. The news sign in the present-day picture shows Phil Bennett, 'the big name in Welsh rugby'.

The Square, Tonypandy during the 1920s, much the same in structure then as it is now, but also giving a clear indication of the extensive transformations that have occurred, as now only two buildings trade as before.

The hotel remains the Pandy Hotel and the corner shop is still a chemist. A brief note of interest on the tram service – in the old days, every tram carried a fleet number and raffles were held to determine which number tram would pass a selected point at a given time.

PANDY SQUARE, TONYPANDY

The Square, Tonypandy, in 1947, showing a secondary school in the centre of the skyline, and the railway bridge running over DeWinton Street. The Pwllyrheboc Railway owned the track that went to and from Clydach Vale.

The large building on the left of the old picture was the Co-operative building, which is now St Andrew's surgery, under partners Dr Robert Baron and Dr Rhiannon Llewellyn. The modern picture shows the surgery in 2002.

The latter-day photograph shows the memorial garden on the site of Cambrian Colliery, Cwm Clydach in 1995. The last major explosion in the South Wales coalfields occurred here on 17 May 1965, when thirty-one men lost their lives. A total of 23,936 deaths were recorded in the collieries throughout South Wales between 1853 and 1974. Thousands more died before the count began. The death rate reached its peak between 1910 and 1919 when 3,748 men lost their lives. The most dangerous era was the late nineteenth century. In 1878 eight nderground miners in every thousand were killed.

Bad working conditions contributed to the heavy death toll; in Wales the death rate was invariably higher than the rest of Britain. Mines inspectors reports show that 3,381 men were killed in the 1870s and 3,045 in the first decade of the twentieth century. Even in the 1950s, the National Coal Board era, there were still 804 deaths. The total dropped to 429 in the 1960s.

Cambrian Colliery closed in 1966 at a time when the end of the coal era was very much in sight. The memorial is a tribute to all Rhondda miners and their families past and present.

Chief Constable of Glamorgan, Lord Lindsay, mounted near the Court House during the time of the Tonypandy riots. When reacting in a crisis situation he would adopt the use of a mounted baton charge or policemen on foot patrol to clear rowdy streets. With a police station in every village, the early guardians of the law were both protectors and oppressors, still the case today.

All police forces are modelled on the London Metropolitan, formed in the late 1820s by Sir Robert Peel, in days when Britain was in the hands of a governing class consisting of the aristocracy and the landed gentry.

The later photograph shows the transition from those early days to the present, now the South Wales Police. Constable Vincent 3707 is a Community Beat Officer from B Division, Tonypandy Police Station, who is specially equipped for the task today.

Nonconformity was central to life in the mining communities of Wales, providing education and religious instruction. Nonconformists were, later, a radical movement in the industrial areas of Wales. The Census in 1851 made claims of superiority due to successful preaching in the Welsh language and the work of the Sunday schools. The teaching and practices of Welsh Nonconformity stood on firm ground in the Rhondda due to a general disinterest in the established church.

At the turn of the century Nonconformist chapels achieved numbers of up to 131 in Rhondda, with a seating capacity of 85 to 103. During the General Election of 1906 there were thirty-three Liberal MPs elected out of thirty-four. Liberal loyalties found allegiance with the Nonconformist chapels, adding strong pressure during the election to disestablish the Anglican Church. Rhondda's history books note it was due to the remarkable Ministry of Canon, William Lewis of Ystradyfodwg, that the Church of England remained strong in Rhondda. In 1869, there were only two churches and two mission rooms, nine new parishes followed and by 1921 thirty new churches and schoolrooms breezed throughout the valley.

Adams Street, scene of the Great Clydach Vale Flood Disaster in 1910. The resulting tragedy and loss of life was caused by the great accumulations of water at the local perch level. More than 800,000 gallons surged through its barrier, killing six people, wrecking houses and almost demolishing a school. Adams Street took the full impact of the floodwater, completely demolishing No. 9, killing Mrs Elizabeth Ann Williams, aged thirty-four, and her baby daughter Frances Williams, aged ten weeks. No. 10 was also badly damaged, resulting in the death of Haydn Brimble, aged just three weeks.

Today Adams Street looks much as it did before the disaster of the floods on 11 March 1910, when at 4.00 p.m. disaster struck the people of Clydach Vale. Rest assured, the residents now live in a far safer environment than their counterparts of yesteryear, due to the water level now being properly drained into the mouth of the Nant Cae Dafydd brook.

The modern picture shows the lake, Clydach Vale, 1999. This area of Clydach is the result of a reclamation scheme, which involved turning a former colliery site, its slag-heaps, miners' cottages, railways and polluted streams into a landscaped area, which is undoubtedly a major attraction for residential and recreational use. There are two lakes, one large and one small. Here can be seen the small lake at the mouth of Nant Clyoach stream; the one on the left of the picture is Bwllfa Mountain, viewed from the Visitors Centre.

The old picture shows Bush Houses, named after Messers Bush and Company from Cardiff. The houses were near the lake and behind towered the mighty slag heaps from the old days when King Coal was the ruler here.

Here is one of Rhondda's best-known boxers – the great Tommy Farr, 1937 British and Empire Boxing Champion. At twenty-three, the former coal miner from Clydach Vale entered the Yankee Stadium, New York, to mix it with world heavyweight Joe Louis, the 'Brown Bomber'. 36,000 supporters paid £265, 753 to watch and an estimated ten million listened to the fight via radio broadcast. But after the fifteen punishing rounds Louis claimed the title on points decision. For many years fans maintained Farr was robbed of the prize.

In the modern picture can be seen, from left to right: Jonathon Jones, aged fifteen, from Heol-y-Drewm Gilfach Goch – with two Welsh titles, he fought thirty-five fights, and won twenty-eight, losing seven; Damon Filmer, aged sixteen, from Broadfield Close, Penygraig – he holds four Welsh titles, the Silver Medal (British) at Liverpool 2002, and has won thirty-eight fights, losing twelve; Liam Williams, from Jones Street, Clydach Vale, is the youngest lad at ten years old. A Welsh title winner, he's had seven fights, all wins, promoted by the Welsh Amateur Boxing Association and trained by Ivor (Pete) Bartlett, also from Jones Street. The Club Coach is Lenny (Lion) Williams, the famous crowned boxing champion from Maesteg.

In the picture below is 'Mabon' William Abraham, who was born in Cwmavon in 1842 and came to Rhondda in 1877; elected to Parliament in 1885, he died in 1922. He was one of the most remarkable figures in Rhondda's history. A Liberal MP for the New Rhondda Constituency, he defeated Lewis Davies through the ballot box and was elected, the very first working-class MP at Westminster. He was also the first president of the South Wales Miners Federation from 1896 until 1912, when his conciliatory methods to problems in the coal industry became outdated and overruled by lodge officials and union members, who regarded a more militant route as the way forward.

The modern picture, above, is of Allen Rogers, MP for Rhondda from 1983-2001, and also a member of the Eeuropean Parliament for south-east Wales from 1979-1984. He was vice-president for the European Parliament during his tenure in office.

Woolworth's, Dunraven Street, built on the grounds of the previously demolished Empire Theatre, and once upon a time acclaimed as the best picture house in the Rhondda. Going to the pictures was a very special experience; for 9d or 1/6d at the Empire you were assured of several hours of great entertainment, two feature films, plus a newsreel and very often a cartoon. The smaller square box and rather bland-looking building is a hyper-value store, replacing the grander Cross Keys Hotel.

The older photograph shows demolition and ground preparation underway in the mid-1960s, with the Cross Keys Hotel soon to be replaced with modern buildings of comparitively little style or tradition.

The shopping centre, Dunraven Street, Tonypandy in 1910, a time when one miner was injured every other minute and one fatality occurred every six hours.

The same shopping centre in 1999 shows a touching acknowledgement of times past; the column is 4.6m high with every millimetre representing a million years in the evolution of time. The black band of Welsh slate is the same thickness as the 2ft 9ins seam of coal in which men once worked below Tonypandy, preserving and interpreting the heritage for future generations of what was once the most intensely mined area in the world.

On the far left is the Dunraven Hotel at the turn of the century; the large construction in the middle left is the Empire Theatre, which was an important musical landmark in Rhondda's past. The theatre put on many theatrical productions, music and film, and also in-season pantomime for the children.

The recent picture shows the old site of the Dunraven is now a neat, modern building owned by the Rhondda Housing Association, with an Oxfam shop incorporated in it. The theatre is now the site of Woolworth's, which is one of the most frequented shops in Tonypandy. This is the main shopping area of Tonypandy today.

The Town Hall, De Winton Street, Tonypandy, built in 1892 and renamed the Theatre Royal at a point in time when travelling actors would come to perform at public houses. By the 1890s permanent, rather than portable, theatres had a greater popular following. The Theatre Royal became famous for its variety and instrumentalists and the introduction of the Bioscope in 1910.

By 1914 cinema had arrived, creating the 'Penny Rush'. Performers of stage and screen inspired people, keeping Rhondda audiences dreaming and living right up to the war years, before the theatre was closed. The former theatre was then used as the main food store for the U.S. army billeted in the Rhondda area. Today, the building is used for office units and storage, with a snooker room and small bar on the upper floor. The basement is a sports bar and nightclub under the name of Woody's. This multipurpose complex was redeveloped in the eighties and situated near the site of the old fulling mill, from which the name of the town is derived.

Theatre Royal, Tonypandy.

Looking South, Tonypandy Square, with the Thistle Hotel on the right, pictured in the 1900s. Zion Methodist church is on the left. The church was built in 1873 and rebuilt in 1915. As can still be clearly seen today, its creation its presence remains strong in Tonypandy. The Thistle started life during the busiest times of the coal industry and played host to Rhondda folk and visiting VIPs right up to the early post-war period.

With more than 70,000 U.S. troops in South Wales in readiness for the 'D Day' assault on Europe, the Thistle Hotel along with a number of other public buildings and private houses made reception arrangements to billet. The Thistle served as the headquarters of the 487 Port Battallion and many officers from the battalion were billeted there. Enlisted men were billeted in the Llwynypia Social and Non-political Club – known locally as the 'Greasy Waistcoat', next door on the corner of Berw Road.

As can be seen in the later photograph, none of the buildings on the right remain. It is now the site of Thistle House, the Department of Social Security and Benefits Agency.

The mill was established in 1738 by Harri David and operated well into the 1850s, serving the farms for miles around. The extension of the Taff Vale Railway to Ystrad in 1855 led to the introduction of cheap textiles from Lancashire and Yorkshire mills, which in turn brought about the decline of the local industry, and the mill eventually closed.

In 1914 an unsuccessful attempt was made to transfer the wheel and the loom to the National Museum in Cardiff. Pandy means fulling mill – a place in which the sheep's wool was treated.

Present times show the site of the old mill from the back of the Royal Theatre. It is now a public car park and recreation area.

The Mid-Rhondda Orpheus Glee on the down platform of Tonypandy and Trealaw railway station prior to their departure for a London concert in 1912. Whatever the Glee men's individual choral preferences, there is little doubt they would leave an indelible impression on the listeners.

The new station here was modernised, in keeping with Rhondda's new roadways and bypass, built in 1988 and opened by the Rt Honourable Peter Walker MP, Secretary of State for Wales.

Lower Dunraven Street, Tonypandy, showing the Wesleyan Central Hall in 1925. The building later became known as the Methodist Central Hall. It was demolished in the 1980s for the construction of a new shopping complex, where Somerfield and Peacocks are situated today.

In the left of the new picture can ve seen the Plaza Cinema. For a tanner (6d), or just tuppence in the 'Fleapits', there would be a newsreel, a B movie and a main feature film, with advertisments and a cartoon at the end – great value!

LOWER DUNRAVEN STREET TONYPANDY SHOWING CENTR

The Rhondda pits strike during the Cambrian Combine Dispute of 1910-11 resulted from deep divisions within the coal industry and in society in general. The experiences over the dispute greatly accelerated the syndicalist approach through direct action. What started as a local dispute over poor working conditions and the problem of no guarantee of a living wage at the Ely Pit, Penygraig, ended with the most bitter conflict in the history of Welsh industrial relations. The problems initially arose over short payments for work being carried out on a trial basis in the new Bute seam by seventy miners. The colliery owner was Mr D.A. Thomas, a Liberal MP, and later Lord Rhondda. His general manager, Mr Leonard Llewellyn, had more than 12,000 men under his control. The company offered one shilling and nine pence cutting price per ton for stone vein in the coal seam. The miners decided to hold out for half-a-crown, but it was in the owners' interests to keep prices down to maximise profits and set the rules for any future disputes in other pits.

As events unfolded, the Ely Pit negotiations broke down and the owners locked the gates. The lock out was very quickly supported by miners striking in other pits.

The South Wales Miners Federation, with leader support in all pits, called an all-out strike; this resulted in no less than twelve thousand miners working for the Cambrian Combine putting their tools on the bar. The scene was set for the militarists. Attitudes rapidly hardened. On Monday 7 November, pickets showing a high degree of unrest surrounded the Glamorgan Colliery at Llwynypia. They had heard news of 'scab' labour being brought in to start the pumps and ventilation plant.

Police stationed at the pit head and out buildings ran out with batons and took up the attack position. The strikers retreated, smashing windows of shops along the Tonypandy main street, and looting rampages were rife. Police continued in full pursuit, driving the strikers under strong pressure from Llwynypia Road in the direction of Tonypandy Square, where a running battle continued with police hitting out indiscriminately, drawing blood with their truncheons. Among the injuries there were fractured skulls and damaged limbs.

The dramatic scene was the direct result of exploited coal miners leaving havoc in their wake. Strikes, combinations and the overall class struggle provoked both fury and fear among influential coal masters and the Asquith Government. Lindsay, at the rank of Chief Constable of Glamorgan, made a strong request for police reinforcements.

The then Home Secretary, Mr Winston Churchill, and two Home Office servants, S.W. Harris and Arthur Dixon, arrived on the scene as confidential officials answerable to Whitehall. Rhondda's smouldering fire had spread to the corridors of power. In the meantime, seventy mounted police and two-hundred foot constables were drafted to the Tonypandy area, with a promise of military reinforcements if Lindsay was unable to cope with the situation.

Captain Lindsay, Chief Constable of Glamorgan, had served with the Egyptian para-military police during the British occupation in Egypt and was a man well known for courting danger. Capitulation was unthinkable; when more rioting broke out near the Glamorgan surface entrance, a directive for reinforcements were called for, including troops under Major General Nevil Macready, a troop of Lancashire Fusiliers, two companies of the Royal Munster Fusiliers and a squadron of Hussars with the Devon troops.

History points to an interpretation of a cautious Home Secretary. The clash of the police batons and the sticks and stones used by angry miners naturally escalated to crisis point, and it was necessary to calm the situation quickly.

Yet Churchill's message to the Stipendiary Magistrates was to hold fast with the application of police force. Lindsay also insisted on this approach, speaking the same language, adopting the same customs, and holding the same opinions regarding the desperate need for military action. On 7 November 1910, he telegraphed a strong request for support.

The War Office quickly reacted to the situation following 7 November 1910. At this point in time the evidence seems to quickly override any historical criticism suggesting heavy-handedness or over-action on Churchill's part. Once he was aware of the location of military troops, he promptly made an effort to hold them back until absolutely necessary, and those troops already placed at Cardiff were strictly put on hold. When rioting was described as having 'gained ascendancy' then troops were mobilised. At the Scotch Colliery a Company of Lancashire Fusiliers arrived. Llwynypia was an area that had already been well patrolled. On Wednesday 9 November a squadron of Hussars was based at Pontypridd, along with a company of the Royal North Lancashire Regiment. Also, 1 Company West Riding was based at Cardiff and 1 Company of the Devonshire Regiment, along with a company of Royal Munster Fusiliers, were in reserve at Newport.

News reports of the day referred to great numbers of rioters being struck down like dogs with broken skulls and left where they dropped. The total casualties between 7/8 November totalled 500 injured strikers and 118 injured police. One miner died from a head injury. Late into the night of Tuesday 8 November there were sporadic outbursts, and the smashing and looting of almost all the shops in Tonypandy. When the Metropolitan Police arrived, Cardiff City Police and the local police force and surrounding police stations were seen to be faced with serious escalation of violence.

Chapter 5

LLWYNYPIA, YSTRAD AND GELLI

Rhondda Sports Centre at the Gelligaleo Park at Ystrad. In addition to the many sports activities available there is the lounge bar and a restaurant with a small café at reception. The sports centre provides very good parking facilities. This Rhondda gem cost the Borough Council one million pounds and opened in 1975.

Glamorgan Colliery, founded in January 1865, is known locally as the Scotch Pit. In 1863 the name of the company was changed from Ely Valley Coal Company to Glamorgan Coal Company, which eventually operated six pits and was one of the top six companies in the South Wales coalfield under Archibald Hood, Archibald, Campbell and Mitchell. The colliery closed in 1945. During this period a number of shafts were left open for effective de-watering and ventilation purposes. When collieries close down pumping may have to continue if there is a risk of flooding a neighbouring pit, and directing and controlling air movement is very important because of gas, dust and fumes, both areas of specialist knowledge in mining.

Today most of the scotch ground has now been regenerated with new buildings occupied by numerous establishments, built in a spread and mixed fashion, with household names: Hutchings – Vauxhall Car Sales, McDonalds Fast Food Bar, Network Q Master Fit, Hyder and Living collections. From this viewpoint the South Wales Fire Service, Living Support Services and Sea Cadets Drill Hall are hidden in the background.

A statue to Archibald Hood erected in front of the Llwynypia Miner's Library and Institute. Rhondda's first MP William Abraham (Mabon) performed the unveiling ceremony on 2 July 1906.

The houses in the modern picture are traditional, built in the early years of Rhondda's growth. Named 'Scotch' terraces, they were one of the best-known schemes of Archibald Hood, one of the most remarkable mining engineers in the countryside during the second half of the nineteenth century.

Miners and supporters assembled for confrontation with blacklegs at the Glamorgan Power House near Llwynypia terraces on 4 November 1910. The Power House can be seen in the background, a little to the left. The experiences of the dispute greatly accelerated the syndicalism of the times through the application of direct action. What started as a local dispute over poor working conditions at the Ely Pit, Penygraig, ended with the bitterest conflict in the history of Welsh industrial relations.

These days the pump house looks in very poor condition, though the structure still remains an interesting building for the historian and tourist alike.

Llwynypia railway station in the early twentieth century. The people standing on the platform are waiting for the up-train to Blaenrhondda at the northern end of upper Rhondda Fawr. In the background can be seen the surface ground, all belonging to Scotch Colliery, which has since closed. The modern picture shows the fine station in place today, along with the sea cadet centre and Llwynypia adult support centre which can be seen in the background.

The statue of the Virgin Mary stands about 1,000 feet above sea level overlooking mid-Rhondda Fawr. The site was the first place of worship in the Rhondda, under the church at Ystradyfodwg, and dates back to St Dyfodwg. Mary's name was placed on 143 churches and 75 wells in Wales, making her by far the most poplar saint. Pilgrims travelled here from abroad in the fifteenth century, to worship and to cleanse their souls.

The dissolution of the monasteries by Henry VIII and the rise of the Protestant faith signalled the end for of Catholic domination. On 16 August 1538 Thomas Cromwell ordered the image of Mary to be torn down and burned in Chelsea, yet people continued to use the site well into the eleventh century.

In 1912 Our Lady of Penrhys was re-established and by 1947 the official status was restored by the Catholic Church, which resulted in the unveiling of the statue on its present site on 2 July 1953.

Penrhys village was founded in 1966 and officially opened in 1968, providing the largest council estate in Wales with 951 houses. Throughout the 1970/80s the village experienced third generation unemployment with all its associated problems. This eventually resulted in crisis followed by migration. The village saw many homes, which had been refurbished under the 1980s priority estates program, placed under random demolition due to lack of demand. This approach saw the village diminish in size. The process of community regeneration began with the work of John and Norah Morgans and the development of Llanfair in February 1992, and the establishment of the Penrhys partnership in 1993. This now ensures a wide range of services and opportunities within the community.

1996 saw the development of Canolfan Rhys arts and education centre, and 'Cartref', which provides much needed, high quality, secure accommodation. What makes Penrhys unique, apart from being supported by so many welcoming organizations, is the long-term commitment of its, mainly local, volunteers to a better future.

Salem Terrace, during the time of Rhondda's first tram service between Trehafod and Partridge Road, Llwynypia in 1908. Some of the locals make the occasion a day to remember. The sight from the wall must have been quite something to witness for the first time. The Rhondda tram company profits for the first year were £22,419, and more than eight million pasengers were carried.

There has been a vivid transformation from the old days, as we can see looking at the same location in 2002, with today's National Stagecoach Express Service.

The Star Hotel, in Ystrad. This was formerly the Gellidawel Hotel. In 1913 it was demolished and the new Star Hotel built up around it. Improved in 1999 the Star Hotel, visible in the new picture, remains impressively traditional, yet boasts all the modern facilities. The road running left leads to the statue of the Virgin Mary, and to the lower Rhondda and Pontypridd.

Gelli Colliery in 1940, founded by Edmund Thomas and George Griffiths in 1877. The collieries on this site encountered a number of setbacks. Five miners were killed and twenty severely burnt when a gas explosion occurred in 1883. The following year the colliery was sold to the Cory Brothers of Cardiff, who sold it to Powell Duffryn Steam Coal Co. Ltd. In 1935, coal production greatly increased and by 1928 there were 1200 miners employed. In 1947 the industry came under the permanent management of the National Coal Board. Gelli maintained a steady level of both production and employment throughout the fifties.

Gelli Colliery closed in January 1962. The greatest number of colliery closures in the South Wales coalfield was in the sixties, when seventy-four mines were shut down. In 1964, man and bulldozer cleared the site for a new industrial estate, creating new employment and meeting the requirements of both large and small firms on the nineteen acres of land, with factory units reserved for industrial use.

Maindy Colliery, Ton-Pentre, opened by David Davies, Llandinam, on Friday 9 March 1866, after fifteen months of craft and patience, and costing £38,000.

The 4ft steam coal seam was struck by the sinkers trust and loyalty. Some £36,000 had been invested and there was still no sign of coal. After fifteen anxious months, the sinkers offered their time for one more week free of any payment and within days they finally struck one of the finest quality seams in the district. Named Ocean Merthyr Coal, 1,220 men were employed at the colliery and 287,000 tons of coal had been raised there by 1890.

After the Second World War the colliery faced a rapid run down due to low economic productions and finally closed under the National Coal Board in April 1948. During the 1950s the site was cleared and landscaped.

The modern picture is of Rhondda's new Magistrates Court in 1999, built alongside Glyncornel Lake, formerly a brickworks established by Archibald Hood in May 1863. The view of the lake above was photographed in 1972. Today much of Llwynypia has a renewed natural beauty, and is a place of scenic walks with access to geological, historical and ecological sites of interest. Glyncornel is situated in seventy-five acres of natural woodland on the upper mountain slopes at Llwynypia.

Chapter 6

TON PENTRE, PENTRY AND TREORCHY

Cory Workmen's Band, who not only rendered beauriful notes during Rhondda's golden era of choirs and bands, but who also epitomised a way of life, rooted in temperance and Nonconformity. Formed in 1884 as Ton-Pentre Temperance Band, they changed their name after the opening of Gelli Colliery library in 1895, when Sir Clifford Cory offered to finance them and sought a director of music for the band to achieve greater national exposure.

Snow-capped Church Street, Ton Pentre, *c*. 1900. The two men are standing near the Welsh Market and Castle Hotel, and the larger building in the background is the Workmen's Institute, now the Phoenix Cinema. The hotel has changed hands and is currently Fagin's Bar and Restaurant. It was a very popular meeting place for Rhondda people of all ages.

Today the more attractive building on the right is Jerusalem chapel. Between 1800 and 1856 the influence of the Church increased steadily; today Anglican Churches and dissenting chapels alike show comparatively little physical presence in Rhondda.

Rhondda Borough Council Offices, Pentre, built in 1882. The offices first came into use under Ystradyfodwg Urban Sanitary Authority, followed by Ystradyfodwg Urban District Council in 1894, and the designation of this body was altered to the Rhondda Borough Council on 30 July 1897.

Rhondda gained its Borough status in 1955 and bears a unique identity well incorporated on the amoral bearings of the new Borough of Rhondda – 'Huy clod na Golud' (Fame outlasts wealth).

Local government did undoubtedly play a significant part in the shaping of Rhondda's history. Rhondda's last mayor was Councillor David M. Rees, the one-hundredth Rhondda mayor. He was inaugurated before the borough ceased to exist and became part of a unitary authority under Rhondda – Cynon-Taf.

Demolished shops and the construction of a skating rink and various public services at Pentre main street during the summer of 1916 was the direct result of a huge land slip attributable to the mining of coal. Without any warning the mountainside seemed to suddenly give way like a pack of 'pyramid' playing cards, which continued to descend on the village.

The slip almost severed the road link between the upper and lower Rhondda Fawr. Afterwards there began the cleaning of the roadways to remove rubble, wreckage and other debris. The District Council made intensive investigations, which resulted in much-needed subsidiary roads being built in the 1920s to try and improve Rhondda's economic and social well being.

Today, the Pentre tips are all gone, and only the lush scenery of the green valley slopes remain.

A pleasant view of Pentre. The mountaintops are part of Mynydd Mardy and Mynyod Eglwys. The photograph was taken on the site of what used to be the Bridgend Hotel, Bridgend Square, once the scene of a violent fight culminating in the murder of the landlord Mr Emlyn Jones by a burglar on 11 September 1904. Eric Lange was found guilty of his murder and was hanged by the neck until dead at Cardiff Gaol on Wednesday 21 December at 8.10 a.m.

Below is a picture of the Bridgend Hotel, taken during the 1930s. The people gathering around the square are probably showing an interest in the photographer.

BRIDGEND SQUARE, TON PENTRE.

A picture of Ystrad Conservative Club taken during a royal visit from King George V in 1912. The writing above the windows patriotically reads, 'God save our King and Country'. Club Stewards Mr and Mrs James are standing in the doorway.

The 2002 picture seems almost to have been taken at the same time. The bay windows have ben replaced with a double glazing, casement frame structure, but everything else looks in place as it always was.